Imm... Materialism

Kathrine Yets

Acknowledgements

I would like to thank local and small businesses, particularly Lela Boutique, as well as Target and Banana Republic for the various retail therapy sessions over the years. By no means do I not appreciate the little things purchased over the years, and I recognize my materialism is by no means your fault entirely, but my own shopping addiction I have created over the years. I would also like to give a shout out to my step father in heaven (for helping to raise me), a shout out to fellow Wisconsin poets (for listening to my rants at open mics), and a shout out to my husband (for dealing with me and my ways the most). I am forever grateful.

THE AUTHOR

Kathrine Yets lives in St. Francis, Wisconsin, U.S. She is an avid educator and poet. Her poetry can be found in various literary magazines and anthologies, including Blue Heron Review, Universal Oneness Anthology, River & South Review, and 5th Wall Press. In 2017, she won the Jade Ring Award from the Wisconsin Writers' Association. She has two chapbooks, So I Can Write (Cyberwit) and The Animal Within (Unsolicited Press). When she is not teaching or writing, she can be found on the shores of Lake Michigan, taking walks with her husband.

Contents

Ode to a Bolo Tie

There are hundreds of options on Amazon,
but I'd rather find you in a thrift shop among
floral brooches, gospel bracelets, brass bangles.
I see you inside a glass display
turquoise center, silver etched swirls.
The frayed leather rope holds you together
cracked with mud between creases,
encrusted in black braiding.

The soil from land in Nevada
where horses, cattle, corn, and hay soak in sunbeams.
Then, you will grace my neck and chest
dreams of banjo twang and cowbell clang
between moos and neighs outside a prairie barn
under a strawberry moon that reflects off the lake
which ripples from bluegill jumps and strider swipes.

This whole world held within your stone
that melds into my bones to create a new memory
of Western love stories
though I know nothing
of the truth
within your knots.

Ode to a Kayak

Oh Kayak flat on the creek surface,
I am tempted by paddles
dipped deep into water,
rippling this placid universe
of blue-green algae blooms and water striders.
Glide, my Kayak, through the sky reflected.
By and by beside cattails, reeds,
and milkweed covered in caterpillars.
Kayak swirled in turquoise and cornflower blues,
your beauty only matched by territory you float through.
Oh Kayak, take me through the twists and turns
to the center of all: the lake's wake
which splashes against your side,
the creation of a lullaby only we know.
Row, row, row to the pebbled beach.
This is not a dream, but our reality
as I wade and pull you to the shore,
wishing time to be as slow as a tree grows,
but our encounter comes to an end
as the sun sets in purple streaks to the west.
This world we created waits in patient admiration
in dewy grass next to the garage
for our next adventure
over fallen maples and rocky currents.
I dream of you until then.

Ode to Body & Earth Gift Set

A student gifts me an ocean
scented self-care kit
for my birthday.
I open it up to find
candle, body butter,
soap bar, hand cream,
and bath bomb
shaped and colored
like planet earth
with blue and green
swirls and masses
like sea and land
in the palm of my hand.
I whiff the lotion—
takes me to the Pacific,
wading in the water
in my little black dress
in the evening moon
hint of sun with overcast
to create a murk lit blur
that only I know.
I come back to now,
appreciate this present
in present, and apply
this memory silk to my skin
that pushes like a wave
back to the past
then pulls me to this moment.
I sway back and forth

as I touch my shoulder
as soft as an anemone.
I know this is for me;
this very second and space
within my body
on this earth.

Ode to Enchanted Garden Treehouse

Take the stone path
to the back to find
enchantments
you dreamt of once
or twice— pinch yourself
because this is real.
Treehome inside
a Honey Locust
that blooms in spring.
Now, a light green
about to turn amber.
On the porch,
we sit and enjoy
rising above stresses
of daily difficulties.
Inside, a vase of
yellow alstroemeria
in the kitchen
invites into the cozy space.
A bed-full of soft pillows.
Then, there's a wooden hot tub
104 degrees ready for a dip.
A koi pond with trickling waterfall.
An oasis outside the city life.
No need to be busy—
relax in this place.

Ode to Lela Boutique

The days get more difficult,
so the soul calls for fashion
beyond the realms of mundane
shopping malls' outlet chains
that are bland and drab—
I'm talking real design
of intricate choice of maroons,
fuschias, magentas of morning
sunrise held within a maxi dress
that beg my eyes for a second glance,
a third peek of the mannequin
until I cannot resist temptation.

Then there's the robin egg,
the navy, the cobalt swag
which drags my body to the rack,
then the curtained dressing room.
To try to choose is impossible
when there's also a tang
of lemon, peach, orange within the trim
and stitch of a single garment.

Praise the emerald peacoats
and periwinkle vegan leather pants.
Praise the floral prints
and newspaper patterns.
Praise, sing hallelujah
for we have found the fountain of youth
within a clothing store in the 3rd Ward.

Go get a silver belt,
some strappy sandals,
a pair of earrings or two
before they're gone.
Whatever you choose, know
that piece of art was meant just for you.

So go forth and shop until your heart
is filled with high fashion,
and you no longer have a care
for the day's strenuous bs
because here you are, looking so cute
that you won't delete it later,
but rather show the world
your confident style decision
of quality wardrobe filled with wonder
and love for all that is vogue.

Ode to The Bedazzled Cow Skull

You were on Etsy
in all your bleached glory
worked to the bone
covered in black glass.
You sold within hours
at $350 cash.
Unknown to me why,
I needed you
with your essence
of rugged life,
yet glamor
inside each reflection
dark as desert midnight.
Now, I search your likeness
across sites
without luck.
Not one captures
your elegance
and crafted choices—
each looking glass
a memory of past
pastures you roamed
in grace at slow pace
without mind to time.
When I look,
the other skulls
simply scream death,
and I cannot shut out
the animal slaughtered

to create a creature
mystical and magical.
Black Beast of the Netherworld,
you were one of a kind.
A true masterpiece
to hide the devilish devise
of a cow's demise
to conjure this art.
If I could see myself
inside the fractured mirrors
of your face,
I know I would be whole
and crazed
to see pixelations
of mortality
crushed and embellished
for beauty to exist
within a world amiss.

Ode to Resin Sword

Is
filled
with
floral
glory of
crisp white
daisy, pink
hydrangea petals.
Then there's the stone
crystals of periwinkle,
fuschia, and sparkles
across your surface.
You are meant for
violence, but likely
would crack
to pieces if a pierce
attempted, yet, still, I hold you, my sword,
toward the cobalt sky as though I'm filled
with power from your beauty strength.
Worth all
1,200 pennies.
You make
me happy,
despite
holding
practically
no purpose.

Ode to Blazer from Banana Republic

Oh you, wowzas.
Making me look so good
with white fringed sleeves
for only 250.
Rock the office
like a boss
inside your tailored cloth.
Size 12 never looked this good.
I put my hands on my hips
just under your stitch
and I dip, you dip, we dip.
Just the right black button
below my breasts,
synching in my sweet spot
to make me look thin.
You are blazered holy.
You are formal glory.
I put you on, and suddenly,
I am a business woman.
I am all that is professional.
Occupational hazard
with how fly I look.

Ode to my Rav4

Blue flame with ice edge moonroof—
you stand out in traffic jams.
Parking structure full of black and silver—
as bold as a frosted tulip in April.
You glide through asphalt terrains
or snow-peaked mountain range.
There's only longings of minutes
within your heated and cooling leather seats.
Only 30 grand to caress my hand
across your steering wheel
and drive through the land.

Targetaholics

for Misty Hadaway

Misty?
Do you want to go to Target?
Stroll around and look for deals?
Company is overdue,
You know I miss you,
Let's get behind the wheel!
We are best buddies,
I love you so,
I wish Target trips were every day.
Do you want to go to Target?
It doesn't have to be a Target.
Let's go play!

Do you want to go to Target?
Or take a walk around the park?
I think hanging out is needed,
I've pleaded, it's time to get away!
We get a little lonely
within our lives,
just watching the hours tick by.
Do you want to go to Target?
I'll be your ride.

Please, I know you're busy,
so many people count on you,
they say, "Misty can you…" and you try to,
but you deserve a break.

We have each other.
It's just you and me.
What do you want to do?
Do you want to go to Target?
I think it's time for Target.

For A Friend's New Year

for Mario the Poet

I pray for you to have endless weekends,
infinite holidays, forever breaks.
To always decide to shake it.
To never have heartache.
I pray your pitcher will always be full.
Your fingers never cigarless.
Your pockets filled with change.
That you choose to not stay the same,
but grow into fuschia magnolia blooms
and azure spotted butterfly wings.
I pray you keep eternal stars in reach,
search for peace, leap in puddles
on rainy streets to plash and splash
all blues away from your thoughts.
I pray you have crispy hot wings,
pho, and THC pickles chips.
That all parties you attend are lit.
That people see grace in your presence.
I pray your bookshelves will be
filled with poetry from friends.
I pray our moments together never end.

Who has the Password to Open Heaven?

inspired by Rick Ollman

Unstoppable and unredeemed,
relentless individuals resent
the world gifted to them—
take and take
and sip macchiatos
then toss the cup
on Rochester Street.
The arteries of the earth
now concrete.
The blood an ocean
filled with plastics.
Dying on the outside.
Rotting from within.
They take and take
and eat everything.
Gorge on desire.
Ungrateful.
Not thankful to God
for this planet.
There's only wait
for gates to open
and the lands to return
to a paradise garden.

The Fall

"my creation myth has no tale of falling" ~Xiao Yue Shan

Oh, I have fallen
down on my knees
to touch glories
I have no name for
other than his.

I have begged.
I beg for Victoria's Secret
body wash and milk and
leather Coach wallets
and other pleasures
that do not last.

Oh, there is a fall—
pomegranate seed
between teeth.
Do I spit or swallow?
I choose to consume
all of life's splendor.
I am a whore.

I have gotten down
to the floor to look up
at the stained glass
only to see his face, only.
Just to feel beneath
and cleanse his feet
with sandalwood oils.
All spirits have a cost.

Guru Musings

The person who yells the loudest
isn't always heard.
Preach on the rained streets of MLK.
Echoes down avenues.
Gospel within each syllable,
punctuated by abhorrent adjectives
of who done what to whom
while those doers dine
on dimes from causality calamity—
make a pay fucking up whole lives
just to buy calamari and steaks
each afternoon for an hour or two.
Expenses at expenses—
how much does a life cost?
Add on taxes.
Put into a report and write off
as charity given to missed fortunes
that were written in each palm—
life lines as slim as skimped joints
or needles.
Supportive services of notebooks
and pens to jot down afflictions
no one looks to see between the lines.
Still, there's Hughes' blue-suede-shoe kinda hopes,
Victoria's Secret's sugar scrub dreams,
Starbucks' caramel macchiato goals,
and all them material things
that fill the voids left by trauma
for a second or two— retail therapy costs

inflated by egos and all those damn
Congrats balloons never blown up
to thank yall for simply making the choice
to wake up and notice holy fuck
we are so fucked beyond recognition
of our own selves with lashes so thick,
nails done, hair did all in vain—
pristine and made ready just for a grave,
buried in credit card debt
and mounds of loans.
Dearly departed, remember
you are more than the Prada
you wore in this life.
Worthy beyond the bills
in leather Coach wallets.
Please find change
to shop local.
To break cycles.
To realize the over abundance of the rich
belongs by natural right to the poor.
The barrier between poverty and wealth
thickens each time a mouth opens
whether for lobster or mac and cheese
or to scream the truths unheard
until they are heard.
and the truth is louder than any ads
for bull shit we don't want or need.
We are fine af just as is.
Fine af.

What To Do When You Only Have 45 Dollars for the Week

1. Attend to your addictions.
2. Buy used clothes for your new position.
3. Buy Ooey Gooey Cake
a. New addiction
4. Sell random things on Facebook Market
a. Red Vase $15
b. Plant Pot Head $10
5. Buy more addiction products.
6. Run out of gas a block from the gas station.
7. Buy gas can.
8. Buy enough gas to make to gas station.
9. Buy enough gas to get home.
10. Call mom.
11. Give mom the rest of your money.
12. Hit up people who owe you money.
13. Never ask your husband for money.
14. Never tell your husband you don't have money.
15. Walk 1 hour to work. Or take an Uber.
16. Overdraft on bank account.
17. Pay bills late.
18. Wait.

Wisdom Removed

I'm suspicious of my wisdom teeth growing in.
Drought my mouth with cigarettes
and chocolates and stress.
I've been trying to do it right.
This fuck-show they call adulting
with $45 in my bank account.
I don't know where I went wrong.

Just call the dentist.
Get the X-rays
and throw away the green glass ashtray
that you forget to empty
so it overflows with filters
and catches small fires
that smells like the bar on Locust Street
after one in the morning
the nights you don't go home.
Throw away a grand or two
on your own health
instead of buying iced vanilla lattes.

I feel them sometimes.
One grows up;
the other sideways
and digs into the molar.
Not as painful as the sound
of my teeth grinding at night
or my jaw cracking.

I'm going to get dry sockets.
I suck cigarettes.
I suck my cheeks when distressed.
I suck on straws for iced vanilla lattes.
I suck at adulting.

The First Shit I Heard

Sometimes our dreams are covered in shit
Or we find shit in our dreams
But we find happiness
Over the checkered picnic cloth
Nonetheless.
Let us be shitty;
Let us smother the moment in shit.
Everything has been so morbid as of late
And I just want you to know
There is shit everywhere,
There is shit on the walls,
But despite this fact,
We should love.
Despite the "shit happens" catch-phrase
On the tip of every tongue
Somewhere south
And north, where homeless hold up
Truths on cardboard posters*,
And the Blues singers and midnight nurses take a break,
We should appreciate the sidewalk and street lamps
After drinking margaritas on Main Street—you know,
Them simple things. Not them material things.
There is shit, yes, a whole lot of it: on the screen of every
Smartphone, in the Victoria's Secret changing room,
Behind the dumpster in Buffalo Wild Wings' parking lot,
Everywhere. Forget your cup of tea idea
Of what exactly it is to step into your dream
Because, honey, this shit is real.

Immortal Materialism

And then there was a wooden stool,
but she didn't have the cash for that,
so she purchased a string of lights
to put on a metal tree in her garden.
There's always a thing or two to buy.
In two days, she has spent
close to one grand on items
she doesn't need but wants
in order to fill a void
with little things.
A hole left from a loss—
her father's ashes have yet to be spread.
Soon, there will be only a jar left.
She bought Aveda hair products
and melon sandals and
periwinkle collared shirt and beach towel
and other pretties to feel better.
She does not want reality.
She wants the materials to manifest
a new life where death isn't truth.

Spend

In pain and weakness, they buy, buy, buy
all materials that bid their idea of a need
when really, it is all cloth and sequins that shines
but means nothing at all.
All will mean nothing in two hours time
when the thrill is long forgotten.
Those jeans fit so nice.
That dress is so slimming.
The lipstick is a beautiful shade of apricot.
No one even gives a shit.
Stop selling out.
Stop.
Spend your dollars and time on memories
not mementos.
Spend what you will not on cheap moments
but rather life times worth of wonders.

Turning 30

I wasted all my energy and optimism years ago,
so please piss off
unless you have an endless
supply of Reese's Pieces
because all that is left at this point
is to get fat and nag at my husband
to fuck me and have children.
But seriously, there is much to complain about
like the kankles and crow's feet.
The midlife crisis coming on early
or right on time
because there is absolutely no way
I will live past 60
with how much I smoke.
This is not a joke:
It is my life wrapped in bubble wrap
and strapped up inside a barrel
being sent down Niagara Falls over and over
hoping for a different result.
It is like a sea otter trying to find the right rock
to love all of life and crack open
every shell to find
it is empty
but wow is it beautiful
and slick with rainbows.
Yet here I am so cynical
and critical of every magazine cover
and checking my vitals—

swear my pulse depletes each day
in this mundane, material existence.
When really, I just need to stop
and look at the red oak leaves
drift aimless towards my feet
and away, which is where I want to be
but cannot unstick my stuck
of this mud pit life I created.
This defeat of materialism
holds me in place
when I just want to drive
and drive and drive
away. Here I am at age 30
with not a single piece to show
besides the pieces of me
scattered on my bedside table,
collecting dust and ash.
Fortuna around my neck
gives some hope that maybe I am
good fortune. I am
able to let go of objects. I am
more than a temporal poet.
I can once again dance
to the tunes already played
years ago on a banjo
and become visceral
with sultry lava skin
that does more than tempt the Gods,
but rather reminds me
that I am whole and holy
no matter what my mind tells me.

Stars

"The intimacy of the stars can be auctioned off" ~Tony Gardner

We sold the stars—
every last one—
in order to pay
for our place
in the universe.
Between cheers and beers
and wine and dine,
we take each other for granted.
We take and take and take
and fill ourselves
with lattes
to fill the voids within.
When really, honey,
we need poetry.
We need an explosion
of fuschia, apricot, crimson, cobalt,
to ignite
fireworks under our feet.
We need the river.
We need the maple and oak trees.
We need the pain, the passions.
To be smacked by a muse
so hard we cannot stop
seeing all the beauty
in the world
and words pour
from our mouths

as we found
the fountain of youth
within our voices.
Let your body move
and jive and jiggle
to the joy of the beats
of your tongue—
the syllables white gold
in your mouth.
Let it out.
Ahwwoooo as a wolf
and laugh— ha ha—
and let loose the sounds
That you buried
within yourself.
Discard your jewels
because, honey, your words are the real sapphires and rubies that
start fires
when jambled together
and jingle with a tongue's tingle to let our screams, our sighs,
our cries, our laughter out so loud it can make kingdoms fall and
damn or salvage souls.
We are powerful beings.
We are powerful.

So Simple

It began without grass or ocean, just a mass
like the inside of a snail shell — murky and moist
and black. Then a turtle crash landed with a world
on his back and laid eggs on a volcano.
The offspring had their own worlds —
alternate universes with timelines askew
of people once known or thought to be.
Each multiverse its own goddess
of venus, moons, mars, earth —
all planets accounted for.
Each a daughter of stone:
granite, travertine, quartz.
A small incision
in the mind
come to find
all is divine
and colorfilled
to the core
like a geode
of cobalt,
mauve,
pink.
Simple
until
it
is.

This whole creation written
on the walls of caves —

a circle here, a triangle there,
a stick person under the stars.
It is. It is. It is.
And forever shall be until
a meteor comes and smashes
into the shell of a turtle
and nuclear war
and plastic fills oceans
and goddess gets angered
and the hieroglyphics on the walls
get wiped away
as foretold by prophets.
All will be as it was:
a blank blanket of darkness
without life.
As it was, so it shall be
for eternity and a day.
Up to the time a turtle returns
the whole begins again
until such time it burns.
Simple until it is not,
and creation turns to rot.
The cycle continues
unless the people learn
to love the earth.

See the Silver Lining

We saw the clouds,
and we saw war—
the smog of factories
filling the air—
polishing metals for weapons
and brewing batches
of chemicals and acids of death
we're breathing in day by day.

The children never
signed for this
when they were conceived.
We walk the patched grass hills
with empty homes and farms
without much hope inside
the children's blue eyes
that dance like marbles
on a washing machine,
searching for life.

Or maybe we did sign for this,
thinking we would find
love and new life amongst the rubble
of what's left
after worlds collide
and collapse
every factory
we created—

the silver lining
in each piece of rusted metal
and swirl of acid
left behind.

Death Toll

Where do we begin? The rubble or our sins? ~Bastille,
Pompeii

Where to begin?
Deaths 20,000 and counting.
A butterfly lands on the rubble
of an old church with ashes
all around— a sign of hope?
Hope feels like a stone on the tongue
when there is smoke choking.
Sin fuels the fires—
a desire, a greed.
We need to do something,
people say and drink their lattes.
Meanwhile, body bags fill
and tanks drive through the streets.
Where to end?
Ukrainian soldiers sleep in empty classrooms
and wonder about tomorrow
with their rifles at their side.
All the red of the day
bleeds into dreams.

Keep Complaining

You complain about gas prices—
just imagine your VW on fire
with nowhere to go
to be safe from war.

You complain about your grocery
bill being so high,
but have you thought
what it would be like to not know
where your next meal will come from?

You keep on complaining
while sipping your lattes
in the comfort of a coffee shop
about prices of this and that
without even considering
what you have.

Be grateful.
Breathe in fresh air outside
that is not full of smog.
Drink clean water
that is not full of ash.
Think of all you have
to be thankful for.

Perspective of A Man Who Drew My Picture

I never planned to be homeless.
That rock just too good—
selenite in the lungs
on the tongue.
What a drug
to ruin me.
Crave night and day.
Each dollar I beg for gone
with a whiff, inhale, exhale
clouds of paint-like fumes
that swirl in grey wonder
one would expect to be calm,
but instead, a swarm of wasps
in my blood who are pissed af.
Words barely form but pour
from my mouth pure poetry
to each stranger on the street
who chooses to listen to me
and not understand at all.
I serve my purpose:
to make them feel better
about their choices
to sip lavender lattes
and wear pencil skirts and blazers
black as an eye.
Oh, how I've seen midnight
moon so lonely as I've been
for a decade within this sin
each person judges, yet here

I am— a smile on my face
despite my transgressions,
speaking in tongues
only God understands
as good as any prayer
from the ones who stare
at me in disgust and pity.
I know what they know not:
These streets are mine,
the very concrete my ground
and I need no thing
to hold me down beside these
Lake Michigan waters.

There And Back Again

Cast your sorrows on him
because he cares for you.
What about the joys?
Give up your jewels and fancy lamps.
Forget the Malibus and macchiatos.
Let's live that simple life
without designer jeans and dresses.
Back to the garden,
naked and in nature,
and stop Eve from ripping the rind
of the pomegranate to crunch ruby seeds.
Stop Pandora from opening the box
and letting out poverty, racism, war.
I want to be holy again,
baptized by the ocean waves.
But here I am with heated seats
and hats to match all outfits.
There is too much.
There is just too much
to go back again.

Previously Published

"Death Toll," *Poems for Ukraine Anthology* (2022)

"Who Has the Password to Heaven?," *Poetry Walk* (2024)

"Ode to Kayak," *Muse Letter* (2023)

"So Simple," *Eternal Haunted Summer* (2023)

"The First Shit I Heard," *Aberration Labyrinth* & appears in *So I Can Write* (2014, 2019)

"Who Has the Password to Heaven," Poetry Walk: Poems of Eco-Justice and Eco-Poetics.

"There And Back Again," *Blue Heron Review* (2023)

"Wisdom Removed," *Rat's Ass Magazine* (2020)

www.ingramcontent.com/pod-product-compliance
Lightning Source LLC
LaVergne TN
LVHW051515170726
843492LV00002B/935